DRAFTS & FRAGMENTS OF CANTOS CX-CXVII

To Olga Rudge

The Cantos of Ezra Pound

EZRA POUND

DRAFTS & FRAGMENTS

OF CANTOS CX–CXVII

A NEW DIRECTIONS BOOK

Number 69—13585

Manufactured in the United States of America

Published simultaneously in Canada by
McClelland & Stewart, Limited.

New Directions Books are published for James Laughlin
by New Directions Publishing Corporation,
333 Sixth Avenue, New York 10014

ACKNOWLEDGMENTS

Some of these poems first appeared in the following maga-
zines: *Agenda* (London), *National Review*, *The New Yorker*,
Niagara Frontier Review, *Paris Review*, *Poetry* (Chicago), *Vice
Versa* and *Stony Brook*. The fragment beginning 'Now sun
rises in Ram sign' is reprinted from *The Letters of Ezra Pound
1907-1941*, edited by D. D. Paige, copyright, 1950, by Har-
court, Brace & World, Inc. and reprinted with their permis-
sion. *Canto XVI* was included in *The American Literary An-
thology/1*, sponsored by The National Endowment for the
Arts.

CONTENTS

CANTO CX

Thy quiet house
The crozier's curve runs in the wall,
The harl, feather-white, as a dolphin on sea-brink

I am all for Verkehr without tyranny
    —wake exultant
        in caracole
Hast'ou seen boat's wake on sea-wall,
      how crests it?
What panache?
    paw-flap, wave-tap,
      that is gaiety,
Toba Sojo,
    toward limpidity,
      that is exultance,
    here the crest runs on wall
che paion' si al vent'
    ^{2}Hăr-^{2}la-^{1}llü ^{3}k'ö
    of the wind sway,
The nine fates and the seven,
    and the black tree was born dumb,
The water is blue and not turquoise
When the stag drinks at the salt spring
    and sheep come down with the gentian sprout,
can you see with eyes of coral or turquoise
    or walk with the oak's root?

Yellow iris in that river bed

        yüeh$^{4\cdot5}$

        ming^{2}

        mo$^{4\cdot5}$

        hsien^{1}

        p'eng^{2}

Quercus on Mt Sumeru

    can'st 'ou see with the eyes of turquoise?

      heaven   earth

        in the center

           is

        juniper

The purifications

      are snow, rain, artemisia,

      also dew, oak and the juniper

And in thy mind beauty, O Artemis,

      as of mountain lakes in the dawn,

Foam and silk are thy fingers,

        Kuanon,

and the long suavity of her moving,

      willow and olive reflected,

Brook-water idles,

      topaz against pallor of under-leaf

The lake waves Canaletto'd

      under blue paler than heaven,

the rock-layers arc'd as with a compass,

      this rock is magnesia,

Cozzaglio, Dino Martinazzi made the road here (Gardesana)

Savoia, Novara at Veneto,
Solari was in that—
Un caso triste e denho di memoria

"Had I ever been in one?" i.e. a cavalry charge,
Uncle G.: "Knew when I came out that
there wd. be one hell of a row
in the Senate."
Knox came in, Lodge said: "Have you read it?"
"For the last time" he thought it was, till
Bettoni, like Galliffet
                    (Ibukerki).
Cypress versus rock-slide,
        Cozzaglio, the *tracciolino*
            Riccardo Cozzaglio.
        At Oleari, the Divisione Sforzesca
        disobeyed into victory,
        Had horses with them.

Felix nupsit,
            an end.
In love with Khaty
        now dead for 5000 years.

Over water bluer than midnight
        where the winter olive is taken
Here are earth's breasts mirrored
                            and all Euridices,
Laurel bark sheathing the fugitive,
                a day's wraith unrooted?
        Neath this altar now Endymion lies

KALLIASTRAGALOS
Καλλιαστράγαλος

 hsin¹

that is, to go forth by day

hsin¹

That love be the cause of hate,

something is twisted,

Awoi,

bare trees walk on the sky-line,

but that one valley reach the four seas,

mountain sunset inverted.

La Tour, San Carlo gone,

and Dieudonné, Voisin

Byzance, a tomb, an end,

Galla's rest, and thy quiet house at Torcello

"What! What!" says the auzel here,

"Tullup" said that bird in Virginia,

their meaning?

That war is the destruction of restaurants

Quos ego Persephonae

 chih³

not with jet planes,

The holiness of their courage forgotten

and the Brescian lions effaced,

Until the mind jumps without building

10

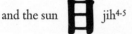 chih³

and there is no *chih* and no root.
Bunting and Upward neglected,
    all the resisters blacked out,
From time's wreckage shored,
    these fragments shored against ruin,

and the sun  jih⁴˙⁵

    new with the day.
Mr Rock still hopes to climb at Mount Kinabalu
his fragments sunk (20 years)
13,455 ft. facing Jesselton, Borneo,

Falling spiders and scorpions!
Give light against falling poison!
A wind of darkness hurls against forest
      the candle flickers
        is faint
Lux enim—
    versus this tempest.
The marble form in the pine wood,
    The shrine seen and not seen
From the roots of sequoias

          ching⁴
    pray 敬 pray

    There is power

Awoi or Komachi,
    the oval moon.

Notes for CANTO CXI

I, one thing, as relation to one thing;
       Yu sees relation to ten.
20 shillings to Wadsworth
              "in resentment." Town house in Hartford.
Roche-Guyon stoned to death at Gisors.
              Power to issue, au fond,
                            to tax.
Directory cd. have made bulwark of Italy
post-bag
              Austerlitz
                     Banque de France
                            Mme de Genlis
Lannes did not enjoy sight of a battlefield.
Whole lesson of Talleyrand
                            Wu
                            Hsieh (heart's field)
                            Szu

Enlarged his empire
              diminished his forces,
Ten years a blessing,
              five a nuisance,
that was Napoleon
with constitutional guarantees
              April 2nd.
"Very few interested"
              N. to Talleyrand, "in civilization."
So that Alexander asked Talleyrand what to do about France.

And "to change the meaning of words themselves from one
conference to another."
Oct. 31st, Wien
And 600 more dead at Quemoy—
they call it political.

A nice quiet paradise,
Orage held the basic was pity
compassione,
Amor
Gold mermaid up from black water—
Night against sea-cliffs
the low reef of coral—
And the sand grey against undertow
as Geryon—lured there—but in splendour,
Veritas, by anthesis, from the sea depth
come burchiello in su la riva
The eyes holding trouble—
no light
ex profundis—
naught from feigning.
Soul melts into air,
anima into aura,
Serenitas.

Coin'd gold
also bumped off 8000 Byzantines
Edictum prologo
Rothar.

From CANTO CXII

... owl, and wagtail
and huo³-hu², the fire-fox
Amṛta, that is nectar
                    white wind, white dew
Here from the beginning, we have been here
                    from the beginning
From her breath were the goddesses
                    ²La ²muṉ ³mi
If we did not perform ²Ndaw ¹bpö
                    nothing is solid
without ²Mùaṉ ¹bpö
                    no reality
Agility, that is from the juniper,
rice grows and the land is invisible
By the pomegranate water,
                    in the clear air
                    over Li Chiang
The firm voice amid pine wood,
                    many springs are at the foot of
                    Hsiang Shan
By the temple pool, Lung Wang's
                    the clear discourse
                    as Jade stream

玉 Yü⁴

河 ho²

Artemisia
Arundinaria
Winnowed in fate's tray

 neath

luna

CANTO CXIII

Thru the 12 Houses of Heaven
>   seeing the just and the unjust,
>   tasting the sweet and the sorry,
Pater Helios turning.
"Mortal praise has no sound in her ears"
>   (Fortuna's)
Θρῆνος
And who no longer make gods out of beauty
Θρῆνος   this is a dying.
Yet to walk with Mozart, Agassiz and Linnaeus
>   'neath overhanging air under sun-beat
Here take thy mind's space
And to this garden, Marcella, ever seeking by petal, by leaf-vein
>   out of dark, and toward half-light

And over Li Chiang, the snow range is turquoise
Rock's world that he saved us for memory
>   a thin trace in high air
And with them Paré (Ambroise) and the Men against Death
Twedell, Donnelly,
>   old Pumpelly crossed Gobi
"no horse, no dog, and no goat."

"I'd eat his liver, told that son of . . .
and now bigod I have done it"
>   17 Maggio,
>   why not spirits?

But for the sun and serenitas
>   (19th May '59)

16

H.D. once said "serenitas"

> (Atthis, etc.)

at Dieudonné's

> in pre-history.

No dog, no horse, and no goat,

The long flank, the firm breast

> and to know beauty and death and despair

and to think that what has been shall be,

> flowing, ever unstill.

Then a partridge-shaped cloud over dust storm.

The hells move in cycles,

> No man can see his own end.

The Gods have not returned. "They have never left us."

> They have not returned.

Cloud's processional and the air moves with their living.

Pride, jealousy and possessiveness

> 3 pains of hell

and a clear wind over garofani

> over Portofino 3 lights in triangulation

Or apples from Hesperides fall in their lap

> from phantom trees.

The old Countess remembered (say 1928)

> that ball in St. Petersburg

and as to how Stef got out of Poland...

> Sir Ian told 'em help

> would come via the sea

(the black one, the Black Sea)

> Pétain warned 'em.

And the road under apple-boughs

                    mostly grass-covered
And the olives to windward
                         Kalenda Maja.
Li Sao, Li Sao, for sorrow

               but there is something intelligent in the cherry-stone
Canals, bridges, and house walls
                              orange in sunlight
But to hitch sensibility to efficiency?
                    grass versus granite,
For the little light and more harmony
Oh God of all men, none excluded
and howls for Schwundgeld in the Convention
                              (our Constitutional
                              17 ... whichwhat)
Nothing new but their ignorance,
                         ever perennial
Parsley used in the sacrifice
          and (calling Paul Peter) 12%
          does not mean one, oh, four, 104%

Error of chaos. Justification is from kindness of heart
               and from her hands floweth mercy.
As for who demand belief rather than justice.
And the host of Egypt, the pyramid builder,
               waiting there to be born.
No more the pseudo-gothic sprawled house
               out over the bridge there
                    (Washington Bridge, N.Y.C.)
               but everything boxed for economy.
That the body is inside the soul—

the lifting and folding brightness
the darkness shattered,
the fragment.
hat Yeats noted the symbol over that portico
(Paris).
nd the bull by the force that is in him—
not lord of it,
mastered.
And to know interest from usura
(Sac. Cairoli, prezzo giusto)
In this sphere is Giustizia.
In mountain air the grass frozen emerald
and with the mind set on that light
saffron, emerald,
seeping.
"but that kind of ignorance" said the old priest to Yeats
(in a railway train) "is spreading every day from the schools"-
to say nothing of other varieties.
Article X for example—put over, and 100 years to get back
to the awareness of
(what's his name in that Convention
And in thy mind beauty,
O Artemis.
As to sin, they invented it—eh?
to implement domination
eh? largely.
There remains grumpiness,
malvagità
Sea, over roofs, but still the sea and the headland.
And in every woman, somewhere in the snarl is a tenderness,

A blue light under stars.
The ruined orchards, trees rotting. Empty frames at Limone.
And for a little magnanimity somewhere,
And to know the share from the charge
                    (scala altrui)
God's eye art 'ou, do not surrender perception.

And in thy mind beauty, O Artemis
            Daphne afoot in vain speed.
When the Syrian onyx is broken.
            Out of dark, thou, Father Helios, leadest,
but the mind as Ixion, unstill, ever turning.

CANTO CXIV

"Pas même Fréron
        mais personne
                pas même Fréron,"
"I hate no-one," said Voltaire
"not even Fréron."
And before Mr Law scarcely 300
        and now 1800 great vessels
and he, John Law, died in Venice in poverty.
                We far from recognizing indebtedness.
                "not even Tom Pick"
"You respect a good book, contradicting it—
        the rest aren't worth powder."

Amid corridors and ambassadors
        glow worms and lanterns, and this moving is
                        from the inward
        o di diversa natura (Giordano Bruno)
and in these triangular spaces?
And is here among serious characters
        and not reasoning from a belly-ache.
Or that Ari. might have heard about fishes,
        thank Alex.
Falls white *bianco c(h)ade*
        yet sentient
                sees not.
Their dichotomies (feminine) present in heaven and hell.

        Tenthrils trailing

caught in rocks under wave.

Gems sunned as mirrors, alternate.
These simple men who have fought against jealousy,
   as the man of Oneida.
  Ownership! Ownership!
There was a thoughtful man named Macleod:
   To mitigate ownership.
And the literature of his time (Sandro's, Firenze) was
   in painting.
Governed by wood (the control of)

木   mu$^{4.5}$

Another by metal (control of)
   Fu Hi, etcetera.

This is not vanity, to have had good guys in the family
   or feminine gaiety — quick on the uptake
    "All the same in a hundred years."
    "Harve was like that" (the old cat-head
      re a question of conduct.)
     "the appointed when nothing can stop it—
     unappointed when nothing can kill you."
Even old Sarah,
   quick on the uptake

snobism — niente —
  the *tribu*.
Armes et blasons!
  me foot!!
Al's conversation — reputed.

Old Joel's "Locke" found in Texas
and Del Mar vaguely on Assay Commission (H.L.P.)
        if it was Del Mar.
Tanagra mia, Ambracia,
        for the delicacy
                for the kindness,
The grass flower clings to its stalk under Zephyrus.
Fear, father of cruelty,
        are we to write a genealogy of the demons?
And on July 14th said:
        "That lizard's feet are like snow flakes"
                τετραδάκτυλος
                (pale young four toes)
ubi amor, ibi oculus.
But these had thrones,
    and in my mind were still, uncontending—
not to possession, in hypostasis
    Some hall of mirrors.
        Quelque toile
"au Louvre en quelque toile"
        to reign, to dance in a maze,
To live a thousand years in a wink.
    York State or Paris—
Nor began nor ends anything.
Boy in the fruit shop would also have liked to write something,
but said: "bisogna esser portato."
The kindness, infinite, of her hands.
        Sea, blue under cliffs, or
William murmuring: "Sligo in heaven" when the mist came
        to Tigullio. And that the truth is in kindness.

From CANTO CXV

The scientists are in terror
  and the European mind stops
Wyndham Lewis chose blindness
  rather than have his mind stop.
Night under wind mid garofani,
  the petals are almost still
Mozart, Linnaeus, Sulmona,
When one's friends hate each other
  how can there be peace in the world?
Their asperities diverted me in my green time.
A blown husk that is finished
  but the light sings eternal
a pale flare over marshes
  where the salt hay whispers to tide's change
Time, space,
  neither life nor death is the answer.
And of man seeking good,
  doing evil.
In meiner Heimat
  where the dead walked
   and the living were made of cardboard.

CANTO CXVI

Came Neptunus
        his mind leaping
                like dolphins,
These concepts the human mind has attained.
To make Cosmos—
To achieve the possible—
Muss., wrecked for an error,
But the record
        the palimpsest—
a little light
        in great darkness—
cuniculi—
An old "crank" dead in Virginia.
Unprepared young burdened with records,
The vision of the Madonna
        above the cigar butts
          and over the portal.
"Have made a mass of laws"
             (mucchio di leggi)
Litterae nihil sanantes
        Justinian's,
a tangle of works unfinished.

I have brought the great ball of crystal;
        who can lift it?
Can you enter the great acorn of light?
        But the beauty is not the madness

Tho' my errors and wrecks lie about me.

And I am not a demigod,

I cannot make it cohere.

If love be not in the house there is nothing.

The voice of famine unheard.

How came beauty against this blackness,

Twice beauty under the elms—

>> To be saved by squirrels and bluejays?

>> "plus j'aime le chien"

Ariadne.

>> Disney against the metaphysicals,

and Laforgue more than they thought in him,

Spire thanked me in proposito

And I have learned more from Jules

>>>> (Jules Laforgue) since then

deeps in him,

>> and Linnaeus.

>>> chi crescerà i nostri—

but about that terzo

>> third heaven,

>>> that Venere,

again is all "paradiso"

>> a nice quiet paradise

>>> over the shambles,

and some climbing

>> before the take-off,

to "see again,"

the verb is "see," not "walk on"

i.e. it coheres all right
               even if my notes do not cohere.
Many errors,
          a little rightness,
to excuse his hell
              and my paradiso.
And as to why they go wrong,
                 thinking of rightness
And as to who will copy this palimpsest?
          al poco giorno
                    ed al gran cerchio d'ombra
But to affirm the gold thread in the pattern
                  (Torcello)
al Vicolo d'oro
          (Tigullio).
To confess wrong without losing rightness:
Charity I have had sometimes,
          I cannot make it flow thru.
A little light, like a rushlight
             to lead back to splendour.

Addendum for CANTO C

The Evil is Usury, *neschek*
the serpent
neschek whose name is known, the defiler,
beyond race and against race
the defiler
Τόκος   hic mali medium est
Here is the core of evil, the burning hell without let-up,
The canker corrupting all things, Fafnir the worm,
Syphilis of the State, of all kingdoms,
Wart of the common-weal,
Wenn-maker, corrupter of all things.
Darkness the defiler,
Twin evil of envy,
Snake of the seven heads, Hydra, entering all things,
Passing the doors of temples, defiling the Grove of Paphos,
neschek, the crawling evil,
        slime, the corrupter of all things,
Poisoner of the fount,
        of all fountains, *neschek,*
The serpent, evil against Nature's increase,
Against beauty
                Τὸ καλόν
                                formosus nec est nec decens

28

A thousand are dead in his folds,
                              in the eel-fisher's basket
                    Χαῖρη! Ω Διώνη, Χαῖρη
              pure Light, we beseech thee
        Crystal, we beseech thee
Clarity, we beseech thee
                              from the labyrinth
Sero, sero! learned that Spain is mercury;
that Finland is nickel. Late learning!
S......doing evil in place of the R.........
"A pity that poets have used symbol and metaphor
and no man learned anything from them
      for their speaking in figures."

All other sins are open,
Usura alone not understood.
Opium Shanghai, opium Singapore
"with the silver spilla...
              amber, caught up and turned..."
                                        Lotophagoi

[*Circa 1941*]

Now sun rises in Ram sign.
  With clack of bamboo against olive stock
We have heard the birds praising Jannequin
    and the black cat's tail is exalted.

The sexton of San Pantaleo plays "è mobile" on his carillon
"un' e due...che la donna è mobile"
    in the hill tower (videt et urbes)
And a black head under white cherry boughs
    precedes us down the salita.
The water-bug's mittens show on the bright rock below him.

[*Circa 1941*]

Notes for CANTO CXVII et seq.

For the blue flash and the moments
                    benedetta
the young for the old
                    that is tragedy
And for one beautiful day there was peace.
        Brancusi's bird
                    in the hollow of pine trunks
or when the snow was like sea foam
            Twilit sky leaded with elm boughs.
Under the Rupe Tarpeia
            weep out your jealousies —
To make a church
            or an altar to Zagreus Ζαγρεύς
Son of Semele Σεμέλη
Without jealousy
            like the double arch of a window
Or some great colonnade.

M'amour, m'amour
          what do I love and
                    where are you?
That I lost my center
                    fighting the world.
The dreams clash
                    and are shattered—
and that I tried to make a paradiso
                              terrestre.

La faillite de François Bernouard, Paris
or a field of larks at Allègre,
          "es laissa cader"
so high toward the sun and then falling,
          "de joi sas alas"
to set here the roads of France.

Two mice and a moth my guides—
To have heard the farfalla gasping
          as toward a bridge over worlds.
That the kings meet in their island,
          where no food is after flight from the pole.
Milkweed the sustenance
          as to enter arcanum.

To be men not destroyers.